THE GOLDEN BOOK OF

MADRID AND TOLEDO

BONECHI

ISBN 88-7009-317-4

MADRID

HISTORIC OUTLINE

In an ancient legend, the founding of the hillside village which grew into today's Madrid goes back to Ocno, son of the beautiful prophet Manto and the god Tiberinus. The story goes that young Ocno is driven out of his native Italian territory by his two stepbrothers. For a long time he wanders, by land and sea, until at last he reaches these enchanting hills, rich in water and green forests. Here, on the banks of a river he founds the city of Mantua Carpetana in honor of his homeland and his distant mother.

The etymology of the actual name, though uncertain, most likely commemorates the abundance of rivers and streams mentioned in the legend. For some, the name Madrid is derived from the Celtic place-name 'Magerito', formed by the noun 'ritu' (bridge) and the adjective 'mageto' (big). Others contend that it comes from the Christian-Arabic name 'Matrit', taken from the antique 'Matrice' ('Mother of Water'), then changed to the Islamic 'Maŷrit'.

During its Roman occupation, the future Madrid was a

small village of about one-hundred inhabitants, depending on agriculture and sheep raising for its sustenance. To find Madrid functioning as an important military center, it is necessary to leave behind those dark centuries of Roman decadence and skip over to the second half of the ninth century, when an Arab prince, Mohammed I, son of Abderraman II, erected a fortress on the site of today's Palacio Real. Arab hands were also responsible for the construction of Madrid's first encircling walls, fitted with robust watch-towers. The oldest and most internal wall separated the 'alcazaba', or fortress, from the 'medina', or city. The other, external wall, with four entrances, ran between the urban Arab agglomerate of not more than 12 or 13 thousand inhabitants and the rural outskirts.

Following two Christian invasions, Madrid was included definitely in the territory reconquered in 1080 by King Alfonso IV. The Moslem presence however, didn't disappear with the Christian occupation. Part of the Arab and Arab-influenced population continued to live in the small Castilian village, gradually fusing itself with the Christian contribution coming from the North. The history of Madrid in the medieval centuries doesn't differ much from that of several other cities in the kingdoms of Leòn and Castilia. There was no telling that only a century later it would become the Court's permanent headquarters and one of the most important urban centers in the Empire.

It was in the 16th century that Madrid and its citizens began to take part in national and European history. In the winter of 1561, Philip II transferred the royal court there from the venerable Toledo. His choice was perhaps influenced by the presence of the reinforcement of the Sierra Guadarrama where the mystic Philip wanted to build a great monastery (El Escorial) in honor of Saint Lawrence, who had guided the Spanish troops to a decisive victory over the French (S. Quentin, 1557). In any case Madrid became a capital for arbitrary reasons, differing in this respect to other European cities like London, Paris and Vienna; it rose on fluvial axes while the others imposed themselves with their demographic weight, heavy economic activity and illustrious history.

In a short time, the population of the small capital began to grow with almost dizzying speed, reaching 50 thousand by the end of the century and more than doubling that of the Madrid of the Emperor Charles V. The Court of the Hapsburgs never left Madrid again except for a short period of time (from 1601 to 1606) in which the weak Philip III gave in to pressure from his councilors and transferred the Court to Valladolid. In spite of the first symptoms of the political and economic decadence of the 17th century Empire, the Madrid of the Hapsburgs continued to expand towards the North-East to the point where during Philip IV's reign (1621-55), the fourth and final city wall was built. When Charles II, the last Hapsburg to ascend the throne of Spain, died in November of 1700 leaving no heirs, Madrid was by then a grand political and cultural center.

At the beginning of the 18th century, the Bourbons succeeded the Hapsburgs, who had ruled the lot of the Spanish Empire for almost two centuries. With the ascension of this new dynasty that promoted important new administrative re-

forms and partially restored the city's economy, Madrid experienced a new unprecedented urban development. This development happened thanks also to the contributions of celebrated French and Italian architects. During the reign of Philip V (1701-46), construction of a new royal palace was begun on the cinders of the Alcazár which had been destroyed by a fire in 1734. Construction was begun as well on valuable works such as the Puente de Toledo, the fountains of the Puerta del Sol, the Tapestry Factory and other great 18th century institutes. Fernando VI (1746-59), continued the building and had the city accurately mapped out. It was however, under Charles III (1759-88), an enlightened and intelligent sovereign, that Madrid finally lost all of that air of a city a bit unsophisticated and neglected through the past centuries. Streets were paved and illuminated by night, sewage channels were enlarged and provisions for water were fortified. The period's best architects, like the Italian Francesco Sabatini, the Frenchman Marquet, the Spaniards Ventura Rodriguez, Juan de Villanueva and others, were called to the Court to be commissioned to design new buildings and to beautify existing ones with splendid neoclassic marble decorations. Madrid assumed a more european and cosmopolitan air, but its demographic growth in the 18th century was slow. No longer possessing a blooming economic life, it ceased to be appealing to immigrants from the depressed provinces and countryside of the Meseta. Up until the threshold of the 20th century, it conserved the characteristics of a parasitic, bureaucratic city that was more consumptive than productive.

The 19th century was studded by wars, fraticidal struggles, democratic revolutions and military pronouncements, bringing an end to the long peace of which the Spanish nation was assured with the Bourbon dynasty of the 1700's. Madrid and its inhabitants were always protagonists in the strifes of that century, above all during the Napoleonic occupation. On May 2, 1808, on hearing the news that Ferdinando VII had been deposed and that Joseph Bonaparte had taken the throne, the populace of Madrid proudly revolted against the 'apes' of the French cavalry, lighting the first fire of resistance to the invaders. This episode, certainly one of the fieriest in Madrid's history, was immortalized by the brush of Goya and commemorated by the obelisk that Fernando VII had placed in the actual Plaza de la Lealtad. During the reigns of Ferdinando (1813-33) and his daughter Isabella II (1843-68), the city was again enriched with new monuments and palaces, gardens and fountains, public parks and tree-lined avenues. By the second half of the century, the expansion of the urban agglomerate surpassed the perimeter of the city's last confining walls, which were then torn down. Today only two doors of this wall remain; the Puerta de Toledo to the south, built during the short-lived reign of Joseph Bonaparte, and the Puerta de Alcalá in the center of the Plaza de la Independencia, built by Charles III. Elegant residential neighborhoods rose beyond the traces left by the 17th century wall, amongst these, the Salamanca and Recoletos areas with their neat network of perpendicular streets rich in greens.

Besides a certain taste for the colossal, there was an

The famous Puerta del Sol. In the foreground,
Madrid's coat of arms: a bear with an arbutus.

affirmed architectonic tendency towards the ecletic, at times
recuperating and incorporating stylistic elements from the
Gothic, Classic and Baroque periods. Expressions of the artistic sensibilities of the late 1800's can be seen in the Banco de
España, the Palacio Linares (the actual Ministry of Agriculture), the Cathedral of the Almudena, the Church of Nuestra
Señora de Atocha and numerous other civil and religous buildings.

In the capital of the early 1900's, tormented by anarchist
terrorist explosions, strikes and social tensions, trams were already circulating, many streets were asphalted and the first
subway tracks were being constructed. In the 1930's on the
threshold of the Civil War (1936-39) the population exceeded
one million. However, a dizzying demographic expansion and
solid industrialization were attained only after the full Franco
dictatorship, from the 1950's on. The working class suburbs
and neighborhoods surrounding the city grew beyond measure
and Madrid was again an important center of immigration for
the poor citizens of rural Meseta Castillana as well as the
desolate, unproductive areas to the south.

Madrid, with its four-million inhabitants and an intense
commercial, financial and industrial life, is a symbol today of
the renewed will and European reintegration of the young Con-
stitutional Monarchy, just a few years after the withering of the
Franco regime.

PUERTA DEL SOL

The Puerta del Sol, is an irregular, polygonal square
in which some of Madrid's most celebrated streets, like
the Arenal, Mayor and Alcalá, merge and form a nerv-
ous center of the city's daily life. The square takes it's
name from the now non-existent eastern gate of the
16th century city wall that had been built more for
customs than for defense purposes. The city's amazing
expansion after its designation as the permanent seat of
the imperial Court provoked the tearing down of the
gate, existing today only in documents and in the plaza
named after it.

The Puerta del Sol owes its actual geometric plan to
the enlargement carried out in 1861, done according to
a drawing by Juan Bautista Peyronet. Many old buildings were demolished and the area covered by the
square doubled, growing from 5,069 square meters to
the present-day 12,320. Luxurious new offices were

View of the monumental Calle Alcalá.

The fountain with the goddess Cybele, ▶
in its namesake plaza.

built under the supervision of the Ayuntamiento of Madrid, which demanded that the building's facades be of a uniform style. The enlargement allowed for the preservation of the antique Real Casa de Correos y Postas, built in 1768 on the south side of the plaza after a plan by the French architect Marquet. This Neoclassic building with a pediment containing royal emblems and symbolic Castilian lions, and dominated by a bell-tower with a clock added on in 1886, was the seat of the Ministerio de la Gobernación (Minister of the Interior) for almost 90 years (from 1847 to 1936). Today the Jefatura Superior de Policia is housed there. A semicircle drawn on the sidewalk in front of the building represents the figurative center of the national highway system; the 'O mile' from which the axes of communication radiate, connecting the Capital with the remotest peripheries.

Today the Puerta del Sol has been transformed into a frenetic commercial center, an emporium in which all sorts of winking shop-windows show off their wares. There are modern cafés, pastry shops, shoe stores, book stores and newstands, shops selling Spanish handcrafts where one can acquire wonderful 'mantillas', 'mantones', and 'abanicos' (fans) and many other items.

CALLE DE ALCALÁ

The Calle de Alcalá, one of the major arteries of traffic flow, departs from the Puerta del Sol, cutting in the direction of the Alcalá de Henares part of the historic center of town and pushes on to the extreme east periphery of the city. The extramural layout of this old country road wound through olive groves and otherwise inaccessible zones and accomodated the first convents and mansions in the second half of the 1600's, when it was given the name it has today. The stretch of road between the Puerta del Sol and the zone that includes today's Plaza Cibeles already had characteristics of an urban street in the 18th century. But it was in the successive century that the most significant civil and religious buildings were built on this route; these include the Palacio de la Aduana (Customs), the Baroque church of the Calatravas and that of San José with its French Rococo influence. During the reign of Charles III (1759-88), in which public works were executed in

many parts of the Capital, the Calle de Alcalá was also decorated with new buildings while the exteriors of others were adapted to the Classical tastes of that period. The Real Academia de Bellas Artes de San Fernando is an example of this. That same period saw the embellishment of two other squares that open onto this major city axis, the Cibeles and Independencia. Between the 18- and 1900's, colossal palaces were built along the Calle de Alcalá, becoming the homes of large banking institutions like the Banco de Bilbao, the Banco Español de Crédito, the Banco de Vizcaya and the Banco Popular Español. The physical aspect of today's Calle de Alcalá takes on many forms; from the ornate Baroque to grandiose City banks, from graceful Neoclassic harmonies to modern 'americanized' office buildings and stores.

PLAZA DE CIBELES

Plaza de Cibeles, the first encountered along the Calle de Alcalá coming from the Puerta del Sol, is without doubt one the most beloved squares of the people of Madrid. In the center of the plaza one finds its namesake fountain, executed in 1781 and designed by José Hermosilla and Ventura Rodriguez, the architects who

in that same period were working on the project for the Paseo del Prado. The fountain's marble group represents the earthly pagan divinity Cybele, wife of Chronos, mother of Zeus and in whose honor the antique civilizations of Asia celebrated festivals and rites of an orgiastic nature. The goddess, symbol of fertility, rides a carriage driven by emblematic Castilian lions. Her gaze is now directed towards the Puerta del Sol whereas it was originally oriented towards the south (Paseo del Prado). The statue of this pagan divinity is extremely popular in Madrid, so much so that there is a proverbial expression that goes; «más popular que la Cibeles» (more popular than the Cybele). Four large buildings surround the square. From the south-west side (the corner between Alcalá and Paseo del Prado), and going clockwise, we find the 19th century building of the Banco de España which was built along Neoclassic lines in 1884 by Eduardo Adaro and Severiano Sainz de la Lastra; the Palacio de Buenavista, carried out at the end of the 18th century by Juan Pedro Arnal on a commission from the Dukes of Alba; the palace of the Marquis of Linares; and finally the Dirección General de Correos (Main Post Office), a colossal Neobaroque building conceived at the beginning of this century by the architects Palacios and Otamendi.

REAL ACADEMIA DE BELLAS ARTES DE SAN FERNANDO

After a long planning phase during the reign of Philip V (1700-46), the Real Academia was instituted with a royal decree in 1751 while Ferdinando held the throne. Academic activity was at it's most brillant after an initiative by Charles III, who secured it a definite place of residence by acquiring the 'Churrigueresco' palace of financier Juan Goyneche. The job of modernizing the building was commissioned to Diego de la Villanueva. The building's façade assumed a pared-down, symmetrical aspect; the sumptuous late-Baroque decorations disappeared, giving way to more harmonious, Neoclassic lines. The Real Academia exhibits a precious art collection, with numerous works from the Flemish, Italian and Spanish schools with several well-known Goyas amongst the latter.

One particular piece merits special mention here. It's Goya'a famous **'Burial of the Sardine'**, of an uncertain date but similar in style to the other Goyas in this gallery which were done in the last ten years of the 18th century. The painting, done in macabre tones and with an air of unbridled liberation of the instincts, is a genre scene representing the celebration of Ash Wednesday. In Goya's composition a crowd of young masked men and women, devilish and smirking, dance under a black flag with the sinister face of the full moon. Here are hints of the stylistic grotesque deformations and caricatures of the 'black paintings' conserved in the Prado.

Academia de Bellas Artes, facade.

Francisco Goya: 'Burial of the Sardine'.

PLAZA CÁNOVAS DEL CASTILLO AND PASEO DEL PRADO

The Paseo del Prado owes its splendor to the artistic taste and sensibility of Charles III, the sovereign of whom it's said found a city of mud and clay and who left it a city of white marble. Spain's best artists worked on the plaza from 1775-1782. The first elliptical outlines were, enriched by three lovely fountains imitating the Piazza Navona in Rome. The **Fountain of Neptune** was sculpted around 1780: the god is represented riding on a giant shell carriage, surrounded by powerful horses and heads of dolphins. Returning to the avenue in the direction of the Plaza Cibeles, one sees the white fountain dedicated to Apollo; the graceful effigy of the god rises from a pedestal decorated with marble allegories of the four seasons. The remaining fountain is the previously mentioned 'Cibeles', now in its namesake plaza.

Plaza Cánovas del Castillo. In the center, the fountain with the god Neptune.

Paseo del Prado: the Apollo fountain.

THE PRADO

The Prado museum is one of the world's greatest galleries with a collection of over 5,000 paintings and sculptures, exemplary of both Classic and Modern art.

Built towards the end of the 18th century to house a natural science museum in the neighborhood of the Botanical Gardens, the Prado is one of the splendid achievements of Juan de Villanueva, inspired by Italian art and the emergent Neo-Palladian style of architecture. Its inauguration was held in November of 1819, on the occasion of the arrival of Mary Josephine Emily of Saxony, soon to become the third wife of Fernando VII. Though all the Spanish dynasties sought to enrich the royal art collections, it is thanks particularly to the patronage of the Hapsburg Charles V, his son Philip II and Philip III as well as the Bourbon Philip V, Charles III and Charles IV, that the Prado today boasts one of the richest and most varied collections of painting in the world.

GOYA

Francisco de Goya y Lucientes was 17 years old when he reached Madrid in 1763. He had abandoned his native Aragon soil where he had had a rudimentary education in the art of painting, and had come to Madrid with the intent of capturing a scholarship to the kingdom's most prestigious art institute, the Real Academia de Bellas Artes de San Fernando.

In Madrid, the young Goya lived out the first burning setbacks of his career. Having failed twice to be admitted to the Academia (in 1763 and 1766), both times without even a point of recognition, in the spring of 1771 he traveled on to Rome. There he managed to broaden his pictorial training in the schools of great Italian art. He returned to Spain and that same year received his first important commission, that of frescoing the vault of a chapel in the cathedral of Pilar. But his real grand artistic entrance had palatine ties. In 1774 Mengs gave him the task of painting the cartoons for the Royal tapestries and Goya worked on these until 1792, with only one interruption.

His pictorial style was formed under the influences of Velazquez, Rembrandt and nature, as he himself frequently claimed. His more notable cartoons are '**The Parasol**', '**The Washerwomen**', and '**Blindman with a Guitar**'. In 1780 he was appointed to the staff of the Academia de San Fernando and in 1785 he became a vice-president in the department of painting in the same school. The following year he got the position of Court painter and in 1789, during the reign of Charles IV, that of the official Palace painter, thus becoming the Royal family's portraitist of illustrious palatine personalities.

Francisco Goya: The Nude Maja *and the* Clothed Maja -
*the two famous oil paintings were done
between 1797 and 1798.*

Here we are at the threshold of the most original period of his creativity, which developed after an unexpected illness in 1793. This period procured him yet more celebrity and economic well-being. The nature of his life-threatening illness is not known but we do know that it deprived him of his hearing and accentuated his tendency towards introversion and pessimism. The first paintings done after the illness, as well as the '**Caprices**' series of 80 engravings done between 1763 and 1796, communicate a gloomy vision of life and humanity. Despite the recognition of his painterly abilites and some fleeting moments of happiness, Goya lived for the most part under the torment of bitter experiences like his consuming, unrequited passion for the Duchess of Alba, her death in 1802, the French occupation, the Spanish War of Independence and the death of his wife Josefa in 1812. The grief caused by war, the episodes of cruelty and violence that he witnessed, the fervence of the Spanish people as they revolted against the Napoleonic troops, all inspired Goya to produce such acclaimed works as the '**Second of May**' and the '**Third of May**' and the series of etchings entitled the '**Disasters of War**'. Tones of dark sarcasm are also found in the last large collection of engravings, the **Desparates** (Foolishness), done between 1817 and 1818. Thematically the series

Francisco Goya:
The Family of Charles IV - *oil on canvas executed in 1780, in which appears also (bottom right) the painter's self-portrait.*

Francisco Goya: The Second of May, 1808 - *This was commissioned together with another analogous painting to commemorate the insurrection against Napoleon by the people of Madrid.*

recalls the 'Caprices' while technically it continues the 'Disasters' series, presenting an accentuated taste for grotesque deformation, caricature, the illogical and the absurd which anticipates the most most fervent surrealist imagery.

In 1819, at this point frustrated by the obtuse and ferocious absolutist regime of Ferdinand VII, he bought a country house otuside the Capital, known as the 'House of the

Francisco Goya: The Parasol - Cartoon *for a tapestry, executed for a doorway of the dining room of El Pardo.*

Diego Velazquez: Las Meninas (Maids of Honor) - *the famous painting represents Velazquez who paints a portrait of Philip IV and the queen, (reflected in the mirror), the infant Margarita and other court personalities.*

Deafman', where he retreated into solitude. Goya decorated the walls of this hermitage with his gloomiest and most enigmatic works, which were later destroyed.

Witches sabbaths, monsters, satanical creatures and disquieting anthropomorphic beings populated these works that became known as the 'black pictures' for their particularly dark staging of imagery and backgrounds and for their qualities of dismay, allusion and anguish. In 1823, the painter who had also kept healthy liberal leanings, was forced to leave his country house to his nephew Mariano and flee for fear of persecution and seizure of his valuables. He went into voluntary exile in France. There he passed the last few years left of his life in the company of his affectionate partner, Leocadia, still dedicated to the labors of artistic creation. He died in France in 1828.

Spanish Painting

In the rooms of the Prado one can review the entire creative scope of Spanish painting, beginning with the murals transfered to canvas that first appeared in the 13th century, up to works from the height of the 19th century. A great influential creative force was that of the

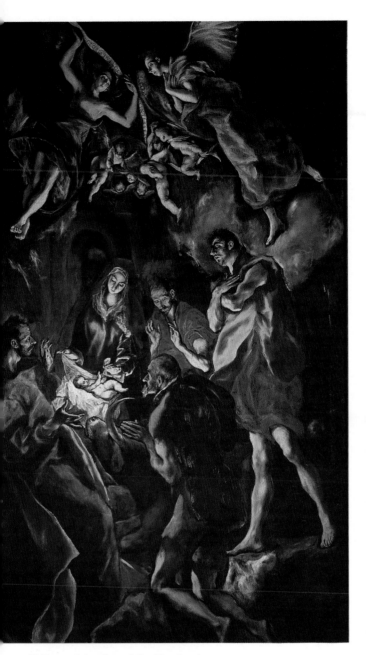

El Greco: Adoration of the Shepherds - *Executed between 1603 and 1607.*

El Greco: Resurrection of Christ - *Painted towards 1594, and signed on the right in Greek.*

◄ *Diego Velázquez: The* Infant Margarita - *This oil on canvas is one of the last works of the master, who died in 1660.*

painter El Greco (1541-1614). He was born in Crete but was trained amidst the culture of Venice and was himself influenced by Roman Mannerism. Always fascinated by the atmosphere of the mystical Toledo where he lived for many years, he created intensely spiritual works. Elongated, rarefied figures, sinuous outlines and faces revealing a tormented sensibility, are typical of his style. Other notable painters are Zurbarán, Alonso Cano, Jusepe de Ribera, Murillo, Valdés Leal and especially Diego Velázquez, one of the most interesting Spanish painters of the 17th century. The early art of

Velázquez (1599-1669) owes much to the influence of 'Caravagesque' realism. Philip IV sent him on long trips to Italy, giving him the chance to broaden his training in the light of refined Venetian art. Amongst his most famous works are 'Las Meninas' (the infant Margarita Maria attended by her maids of honor), the 'Surrender of Breda' and 'Las Hilanderas' (the spinners). The Prado also houses the almost complete works of Francisco Goya (1746-1828), including the mural paintings, later transfered to canvas, from his 'Houses of the Deafman'.

Pieter Brueghel: The Triumph of Death - done towards 1564, the painting was inspired by the riots caused by Spanish oppression in the Low Countries.

Flemish paintings and tapestries woven by skilled Belgian craftsmen. Many masters from the other side of the Alps came to Spain, attracted by the available gold of its princes and royalty. Here, Flemish painting was in fashion from the end of the 15th century to well into the 1800's. Paintings by Jan van Eyck, Roger van der Wyden, and Hans Memling were appealing for their concrete descriptive qualities, realistic detail, acute psycological penetration and sense of color. But Flemish painting didn't mean just bourgeois settings, scenes of rural life and faithful portraits; there's Hieronymous Bosch, whose celebrated 'Hay Wain' and 'Garden of Earthly Delights' are in the Prado. Bosch was a master of fantastic, hallucinatory vision with deep sym-

Flemish Painting

Thanks to the strict ties that existed for around one and a half centuries between the Spanish empire and the Low Countries (Netherlands, Belgium and Luxembourg), the royal residences of the Hapsburgs were enriched with

Rogier van der Weyden: Descent from the Cross - this tempera on wood was the central part of a triptych of which the lateral panels have been lost.

16

bolical values. The painting of Pieter Bruegel the Elder is also enigmatic and disquieting, thick in meaningful allegory despite its appearance of corporal realism. The Flemish painter with the greatest presence of paintings in the Prado however, is Peter Paul Rubens. He maintained in fact, a very lively rapport with the Spanish royalty and was a resident of the court of Philip IV of Hapsburg from 1628 to '29. Some of his more beatiful paintings, with their great color effects, are, the 'Pietà', 'Diana the Huntress' and the 'Judgement of Paris'.

Italian Painting

Many paintings from the Italian school were acquired for the Spanish royal collection by the emperors Charles V, his son Philip II and the cultured Philip IV, who consulted Velázquez for the major part of his acquisitions. The refined Venetian painting that appealed so to the Spaniards, is represented by paintings by Tintoretto, Veronese, Bassano, Mantegna and by Titian, who did two splendid portraits of Charles V. One of these, the 'Equestrian portrait' of 1548 represents the sovereign during his victorious Battle of Mülhberg in April of 1547. There are also numerous paintings by Giovan Battista Tiepolo and his son Gian Domenico, luminaries of Venetian painting particularly favoured by Charles III of Bourbon. Alongside

the Venetian masters, the Prado exhibits paintings by many other Italian artists, from the spiritual painting of Botticelli, influenced by Marsilio Ficino and Pico della Mirandola, to the soft Virgins of Raphael and the crude realism of Baroque painting.

Hans Memling: Adoration of the Magi - *painted towards 1470, the side panels of the triptych represent the Nativity and the Purification.*

Titian: Charles V on Horseback - *Large canvas executed in 1548 to commemorate the victorious battle of Mühlberg.*

*Casón del Buen Retiro. View from the west side,
a work of Ricardo Velázquez Bosco (1891).*

THE CASÓN DEL BUEN RETIRO

The Casón, surrounded today by asphalt, was once surrounded by luxuriant greens, when it was still a residence of Philip IV. It was added to the Palacio del Buen Retiro in 1638 to provide more space to be dedicated to Court parties and sumptuous receptions. This was an era of crisis and decadence in Madrid. The reaction to this was a taste for artifice, and extravagance as well as bizarre inventions: anything that served to give an illusion of splendour that was by this time lost. For the celebration of important royal family events such as births, birthdays and weddings, or for the reception of worthy foreign princes and kings, the Buen Retiro was transformed into a sumptuous party scene complete with fireworks, games, and spectacles. Sometimes a stupified public was let in to watch. But the illusion faded like a dream. The aggravation of the political and economic crises of the end of the century brought on the decline of the royal complex of the Buen Retiro as well. Charles II, Spain's last Hapsburg, working with scarce financial means, decided to save just the Casón from the ravages of time, for which he

then commissioned decorative frescoes by the prolific Napolitan painter Luca Giordano. Having survived the destructive War of Independence together with the north wing of the Palacio (now the Museo del Ejercito or Army Museum), the Casón served in the 19th century as a topography workshop, a riding school for King Alfonso XII of Bourbon and then as a museum of artistic prints. Today the Museo de Arte Español del Siglo XIX is installed there, a fundamental collection of Spanish painting from the Romantic, Realist and Impressionist periods. The Casón del Buen Retiro has recently acquired one of Picasso's masterpieces, **'Guernica'**, exhibited until very recently in New York's Museum of Modern Art.

This picture was painted in the spring of 1937, following the bombing of the small Basque town by the German air forces in an alliance with Franco's troops. The painting, thick with mythological symbolism, expresses horror at this triumph of barbarism and pure bestiality through a figurative chaos, the decomposition of the forms and a palette of predominant sullen grays.

PLAZA DE LAS CORTES

A short distance from the Plaza Cánovas del Castillo, between the Carrera de San Jeronimo and the graceful Plaza de las Cortes, rises a large Neoclassic building, which has been the seat of Parliament since the second half of the 19th century. The palace was built during the reign of Isabella II, from 1843 to 1850, after the plan by Pascual y Coloner. The most interesting façade, with a six-columned portico and Corinthian capitals, is that which looks out onto the Plaza de las Cortes. An allegorical bas-relief is sculpted into the pediment; two central female figures, representing Spain and the Constitution are surrounded by other moving and equally symbolic figures. These latter represent incarnations of the arts, the professions and concepts such as Peace and Prosperity. Two bronze lions by the sculptor Ponciano, flank the grand entrance staircase. These were cast from the melted-down enemy cannons that the Spanish had captured during the Moroccan military campaign of 1859-60. At the center of the square, surrounded by plants and flowerbeds, rises the monument dedicated to the celebrated Spanish storyteller Miguel de Cervantes. The monument was designed by the sculptor Antonio Sala in the first decade of this century.

The monument to Miguel de Cervantes in the Plaza de las Cortes.

The principal facade of the House of Parliament, seen from the Plaza de las Cortes.

MUSEO DEL EJERCITO
(Army Museum)

The idea of founding a large armory, a place in which to collect the relics and testimonial pieces of Spain's military glories, came towards the beginning of the 19th century to Manuel Godoy. Godoy was an obscure officer in the Royal Guard who had ascended to the heights of political power thanks to the favors of his mistress Maria Luisa of Parma, wife of the complaisant Charles IV. The collection of arms and trophies had been put up in various buildings throughout the city until it found a final seat in the north wing of the Hapsburg residence 'Buen Retiro', its only surviving wing together with the 'Casón' and its namesake park. In the museum's rooms, which, include the sumptuous **'Salón de Reinos'**, are exhibited relics, standards and military equipment of every type, from the swords that were unsheathed by Medieval warriors against Moors

*Museo del Ejército:
interior staircase.*

*Museo del Ejército:
the sumptuous Salón de Reinos.*

and traitors, to the firearms, used during the last Spanish civil war.

Centuries of conflict and bloody battle parade before our eyes like a wondrous projection that overshadows the throngs of anonymous soldiers that forged Hispanic destiny. It only took the shaking of a leader's or sovereign's fist to initiate a challenge to the threat of oblivion and there are relics to commemorate these undertakings; the swords of the Castilian nobles Quiñones and Diego de Mendoza, the standard of the conquerer Hernán Cortes, the tent and military insignia of Charles V and much more. Also of great interest are the scale models and reproductions showing methods of fortification, campsites and the various equipment of war.

Two more beautiful rooms in the Museo del Ejército.

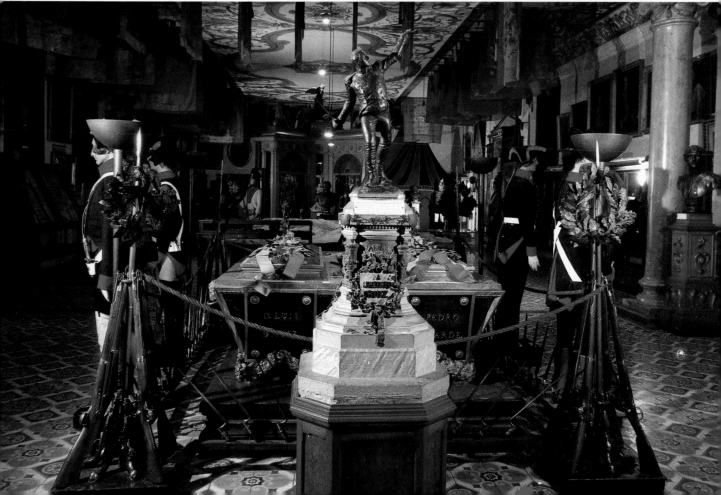

JARDIN BOTANICO
(Botanical Garden)

The birth of a luxuriant botanical garden within the grounds of the 'Buen Retiro' is proof of nature's role in the 18th century of being more than just a source of delight and relaxation. A new sort of vegetation rose, different from formal pleasure gardens in that the plants were objects of study and systematic cataloging. Designed by Juan de Villanueva, the Botanical Garden was inaugurated during the reign of Charles III. It was part of a group of schools including those of physics, chemistry, medicine and astronomy which little by little formed the project for a major university; something lacking in the Capital. The incrementation of the garden's vegetation was made possible thanks to scientific expeditions promoted and subsidized by Charles III, donations from foreign botanical gardens and above all, to an arrangement that emanated from the same king, requiring the governments of the American provinces to periodically send examples of their indigenous plants to the institute.

A foreshortening of the Botanical Gardens.

Estación Atocha. (The Atocha Station)

Inside the Garden, marked out by an elegant cast iron fence with two Neoclassic gates by Villanueva, rose the pavillion destined to become the university's school of botany and its library. Up to a few years ago, the public could benefit from this cultivation of the most disparate of medicinal herbs. Continuing a tradition established by Charles III, plants and cuttings were openly distributed, for the making of medicinal decoctions, infusions and rubs.

PLAZA DE LA INDEPENDENCIA

In the north-east zone of the Capital, between the elegant Recoletos quarter and the Retiro park, lies the 19th century Plaza de la Independencia, so named to commemorate the Spanish people's victory in the war against Napoleonic forces (1808-13). The square rose up around the Puerta de Alcalá after the last city wall was torn down in the course of the 19th century to make room for the constantly expanding urban agglom-

erate. The square's most significant monument is the above-mentioned gate, built between 1769 and 1778 by the Italian architect Francesco Sabatini, as desired by Charles III. The ex-king of Naples, utilizing the genius of the epoch's architects and sculptors, brought splendid Neoclassic improvements and modern, more rational city-planning to the Capital. The gate was erected over the ruins of 17th century arch that had been a richly decorated Baroque monument erected during the reign of Philip III (1598-1621), to honor his first wife, Margaret of Hapsburg.

Sabatini reached the final plans after a long phase of preparation. It was initially conceived as having five vertical elements, but with only four arches, two rounded ones and a pair of vaulted exterior ones. In the final drawing the gate was improved by the addition of a fifth centrally placed round arch, and also by the elimination of a heavy ledge that projected horizontally from the arches. The more majestic external facade is ornamented by ten Ionic columns and a curvilinear pediment with an inscription of the name of King Charles and the year of its termination, as well as with sculptures by Michels similar to the cornucopias he sculpted onto the exterior's vertical elements.

The majestic Puerta de Alcalá,
in the center of the Plaza de la Independencia.

JARDINES DEL RETIRO
(Retiro Park)

The Retiro Park, which extends for over 40 acres, between the Calle de Alcalá, Calle de Alfonso XII and the Avenida de Menéndez y Pelayo, is one of the city's great green oases. Along with the Museo del Ejercito and the Casón del Retiro, it's all that remains of the old Hapsburg residence. It was built near the monastery of Saint Jerome between 1631-32 for the young Philip IV. It was to the palace called Buen Retiro (pleasant retreat), that the sovereigns retreated in pensive solitude, during important religious solemnities such as Holy Passion Week, official mourning periods or just to fortify themselves. The residence was abandoned in the second half of the 18th century when Charles III established residency in a wing of the Palacio de Oriente. Although reduced in size, the park has survived the years, and in 1868, it became municipal property. There are many fountains, reflecting pools, flowerbeds and monuments adorning the park, making it an ideal place for charming strolls and a pleasant divertisement. Outstanding monuments include those to the histologian Ramón y Cajal, Nobel prize winner in 1906, and the realist story-teller Benito Pérez Galdos, both by the sculptor Victorio Macho. Others honor King Alfonso XII, the musician Chapí and the Alvarez Quintero brothers, celebrated comedy-writers of this century. Surrounding the large reflecting pools in the park's center, are the 18th century Exposition and Crystal palaces.

A boatride on the Retiro's lake. In the background, the equestrian monument to King Alfonso XII.

A graceful corner of the Retiro.

◀ *Neoclassic beauty in the Parco del Retiro.*

◀ *The Retiro's elegant Crystal Palace.*

BIBLIOTECA NACIONAL (NATIONAL LIBRARY) AND MUSEUMS

The Biblioteca Nacional didn't have a permanent seat until the 19th century. The pseudo-classic building hosts a collection of almost four million volumes, plus rare manuscripts and precious incunabula. It was built after a design by the architect Ruiz de Salaces in the threshold of this century, to house a grand exhibition for the four-hundred year anniversary of the discovery of America and to provide a permanent and adequate seat for Spain's most prestigious library. The establishment of the first public library goes back to the age of Philip V. In March of 1712, utilizing books and manuscripts that were royal property, Philip opened a library that was reserved to male citizens. Access to it continued to be forbidden to women until 1838 and the reign of Maria Cristina. A law promulgated by Philip V, required editors to donate a copy of every one of their

Above, the facade of the Biblioteca Nacional; Museo Arqueológico, ivory Crucifix, a votive crown, the Dama de Baza and jewels from the Treasure of Aliseda.

publications to the library. Thanks to this law, the library's holdings have been gradually enriched with the latest books from the 18th century on up to our own times.

The Biblioteca Nacional building has played host until very recently, to the important museums of Modern and Contemporary art which have since been transfered to the Casón del Buen Retiro and the Ciudad Universitaria. What remains is Spain's greatest archaeological museum, the Museo Arqueologico Nacional, founded by Isabella in 1867. In the gardens facing the museum's entrance on the Calle de Serrano, are reproductions of the splendid prehistoric **Altamira** cave paintings. In the collection of Iberian art, the most famous pieces are; the '**Dama de Elche**', a statue of an antique Iberian divinity from the fifth century B. C.; the '**Dama de Baza**', a fourth century B. C. statue representing the goddess of Death and Rebirth; and the '**Treasure of Aliseda**'. The precious objects of the Aliseda date back to the seventh century B. C. and show Phoenician and Oriental influence. Of notable interest also is the '**Treasure of Guerrazar**', consisting of the Visigothic king's beautiful collection of gold votive crowns encrusted with jewels; and an 11th century **ivory crucifix** from the church of San Isidro de Leon.

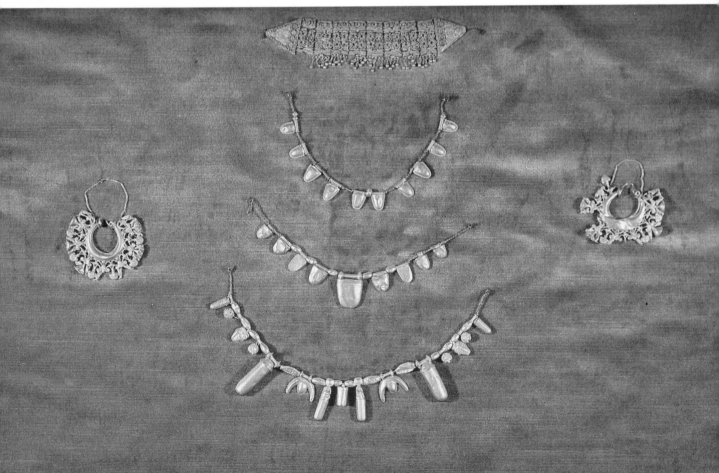

CENTRO CULTURAL DE LA VILLA DE MADRID

The Descubrimiento gardens in the modern Plaza de Colon; the sculpture in memory of the discovery of America and the monument to Christopher Columbus.

PLAZA DE COLÓN

Situated on the intersection of four grand urban arteries, including the Paseos de Recoletos and de la Castellana, it is one of the Capital's more modern plazas. It lost its 1700's aspect just recently thanks to work done to restructure and enlarge it, carried out in the 1960's.

The beautiful Descubrimiento gardens, which open out on the east end of the plaza, have taken the place of the old Mint, a building from the period of Isabella II, that was demolished a few years ago. The square's most admirable monument is certainly the 1886 **statue** by the sculptor Arturo Mélida, holoring **Christopher Columbus**. The marble sculpture of the navigator rises from a Neogothic pedestal, consisting of three elements gradually diminishing in size, about seventeen yards high. Parking lots and underground pavillions have almost doubled the already vast area of the square. Underground there are shops and exhibition halls.

Church of the Salesas Reales: the principal facade.

Instituto Valencia: the outside and two interior views. ▶

THE CHURCH
OF SAINT BARBARA

Tormented by an obsession with death and the terror of an early widowhood, the Portugese Princess Barbara of Braganza, wife of the king Fernando VI of Bourbon, wanted to assure herself of a refuge for the event and built a convent outside the modern day Plazas de la Villa and de las Salesas. The project was given to the French architect Carlier who began work in 1750, but the job was finished by the Spaniard Francisco Moradillo between 1756 and 1758. The church, rising next to a convent reserved to an order of Salesian nuns, is in the form of a Latin cross with a central dome and French Rococo elements that fuse themselves with Spanish Baroque decorations. Abandoning the granite and red tiles that were favored in proceeding epochs, Carlier and Moradillo used precious Italian and Spanish marbles which came from Genoa, Granada and Cuenca. The church's façade, despite its eight ornamental pilars and the two lateral towers added by Moradillo, doesn't give an impression of upward flight, the pronounced horizontal cornice breaking up the sense of rhythmic ascension. The inside of the temple houses the marble tombs of its founders, Barbara of Braganza and Ferdinand VI. The tombs were designed by the Italian Sabatini but executed by Francisco Gutiérrez during the reign of Charles III (1759-88). The queen, who had ardently wished to spend the last years of her life in the convent, fulfilled that wish only after her death and the ensuing eternal rest.

Towards 1870, the State alienated the monastery from the order of the Royal Salesians and adapted it to civil use. From that point on it has been the seat of various judicial bodies. The church today is part of the parish of Saint Barbara.

MUSEO VALENCIA
DE DON JUAN

An interesting collection of art housed in a Moorish style building on Calle Fortuny, on the outskirts of the majestic Paseo de la Castellana. There are numerous ceramics, tapestries, arms, furnishings, coins and jewels from varying styles and sources gathered here thanks to the sensibility and money of the noble Guillermo de Osma and his wife, the Countess Valencia de Don Juan. Of the objects exhibited, the ones meriting particular attention are the valuable collection of 'azulejos', Medieval majolica tiles in the Moorish style, Compostelan jet carvings, an emerald dragon belonging to Hernán Cortés and offered by him to the Virgin of Guadalupe, an El Greco and other important paintings.

◀ *Partial view of the Plaza Mayor; bottom, the equestrian monument of Philip III of Hapsburg.*

Aerial view of the Plaza Mayor.

PLAZA MAYOR

The project-plan to build a plaza between the old walls of Madrid, corresponding to the Guadalajara gate and the encircling 15th century wall, goes back to the reign of Philip II (1556-1598) and is the work of the great Juan de Herrera, the major craftsman of the monastery of Escorial. Work was begun in 1590 and completed by the architect Juan Gómez de Mora during the last years of Philip III's life (1617-20), who wanted to attribute to it the name it still bears today. The plaza, with nine entrances surmounted by rounded arches and three rows of more than four-hundred balconies ornamented with graceful wrought-iron railings, assumed its present aspect after various restorations and embellishments; the rebuilding of the southern and northern sides after their devastation by fires in 1671 and '72, the Neoclassic improvements of the end of the 18th century by Juan de Villanueva, and the installation in the center of the plaza of the equestrian '**Statue of Philip II**'. The monument was cast in Florence by Giambologna after a model by the Tuscan sculptor Pietro Tacca and transported to Madrid in 1616. It was first placed amidst the green of the Real Casa de Campo, where it remained until 1848, when Isabella II decided to transfer it to the center of the Plaza Mayor. On the south side, between two towers topped by high pinnacles, we find the most interesting building in the plaza, the Real Casa de la Panadería, begun by Sillero and carried out to its finish by Gómez de Mora. While the ground floors were occupied by the royal bakeries (hence its name), the second floor apartments were occupied by the rulers during grand events in the political, social and religious life of the city. From the balconies that look out onto the plaza, the royals took part in solemn executions of criminals, the canonization of sanits such as the Capital's patron saint San Isidro in 1622, theater, bullfights and splendid civil and religious ceremonies. The plaza has long since become a grand pedestrian isle, a gathering place for madrilens and tourists. There they admire it's beauty and sober architecture while seated in cafes or they crowd into the shops that line its porticoes. Sunday mornings it becomes the habitual meeting place for those with a passion for stamp-collecting. They come in search of that rarity or new collector's item, in the Stamp Market that is set up under the porticoes in the south side of the plaza.

Principal facade of the Ministry of Foreign Affairs, with its beautiful portal of Italian influence.

Cathedral of San Isidro: exterior. ▶

MINISTRY OF FOREIGN AFFAIRS

The building in the Plaza de la Provincia that has been the seat of the Foreign Affairs Minister since 1931, was once one of the places most feared and hated by any citizen having outstanding business with the courts. It began as the Court Prison, as desired by Philip IV, between 1629 and 1662, the year in which the architect José de Villarreal concluded work on it. The initial project was by Juan Gómez de Mora but the building was realized almost entirely by Cristóbal de Aguilera, even if it continues to be erroneously attributed to the Italian, Giovambattista Crescenzi. The prison was partially rebuilt during the reign of Charles III by Juan de Villanueva, to repair the damages to it caused by a raging fire in 1791. The building ceased to function as a penitentiary towards the middle of the 19th century, when for some years it was the seat of Parliament.

Despite work on it in the 17th century, its architectural lines are of an austere and rigorous Classical style. The principal facade, facing the Plaza de la Provincia, is ornamented by two beautiful peaked towers typical of Madrilene civilian architecture and an elegant portal of

Italian influence, topped by a pediment with the heraldic insignia of the Spanish Crown. The external Tuscan style columns are perfectly identical to those in the two large symmetrical interior courtyards around which develops the rectangular plan of the building. The courtyard's columns, united by curved arches and enriched by Doric friezes and Classical stone masks, are examples of a rare harmony and decorative simplicity.

CHURCH OF SAN ANDRÉS

To the south-west of the Plaza Mayor, in one of the oldest and most characteristic quarters of Medieval Madrid, rise the church of San Isidro, in a unique architectural complex. The ancient temple, erected in the medieval era in the place where, according to legend, the remains of San Isidro, Madrid's patron saint were buried, hasn't survived the wear and tear of time. Towards the middle of the 17th century, Philip IV decided to have a church built on the ruins and to embellish it with a chapel dedicated to the patron saint destined to accomodate it's venerable relics. Carried out by Pedro de la Torre and José de Villareal, with an octogonal floor plan, supported vaults and a slate dome, the chapel was ornamented with stuccoes and rich Baroque decoration. It was later destroyed during the three years of the Civil War and then only partially restored. The remains of San Isidro were transfered in 1769, according to the wishes of Charles III, to his namesake cathedral where they have been kept to this day.

CATHEDRAL OF SAN ISIDRO

On the present day Calle de Toledo, a short distance from the church of San Andrés, is the cathedral of the Society of Jesus, the order founded by Ignacio de Loyola, built between 1622 and 1660. Despite successive alterations and damages suffered during the Civil War, the Jesuit temple, designed by Francesco Bautista and Pedro Sánchez, has conserved many of its original characteristics, such as its one main nave, its Latin-cross floor plan and Baroque interior decorations. In 1767, during the reign of Charles III, the Jesuits were expelled from Spanish territory, suspected of stirring up populace sentiments against the reformist ministers favoured by the King. The cathedral, modernized by Ventura Rodriguez, has since then housed the remains of San Isidro, patron saint of Madrid and protector of crops. Today it still houses the saint's tomb and was restored to its ancient splendor just a few decades ago.

Church of San Andrés. View outside the chapel of San Isidro and the Baroque interior.

◄The Alcazar and the Alcántara bridge.

The north façade of the Alcazar.

Bonaparte's armed forces. The fire raged for three days and three nights. It was then rebuilt between 1867 and 1882, when the building was converted into the Military Infantry Academy.

The last disaster dates back to the XXth century. When the Spanish Civil War broke out, the Commander of the «Escuela General Gimnasia de Toledo», José Moscardó Ituarte, prevented from directly joining the insurgents, assembled the troops supporting General Franco's uprising in the Alcázar, thus establishing a nationalistic nucleus in the rampart of Toledo. The Republican troops did not waste time taking a stand and pre-pared a siege that lasted 72 days, during which time almost the entire building was destroyed. Not only soldiers and officers were besieged, but also women and children. On that occasion, General Moscardó chose to sacrifice his son rather than surrender to the enemy. The besieged managed to hold the fort until General Varela's troops arrived. This episode is documented in detail in the halls of the present day Alcázar, which was rebuilt along the lines of the previous project. On leaving the Alcázar, one can admire a monument dedicated to the city's defenders during the siege attributed to Juan de Avalos.

Another view of the Alcazar.

The central courtyard of the Alcazar with the monument to Charles V (copy by L. Leoni).

Alcazar, bust of the Commander José Moscardó Ituarte and evidence of the Civil War.

Plaza de la Villa (or del Ayuntamiento) with the Town Hall and Archbishop's Palace.

The main façade of the Cathedral.▶

LA PLAZA DEL AYUNTAMIENTO

Also known as Plaza de la Villa, it is flanked to the south by the Town Hall and Law Court, to the west by the Archbishop's Palace and to the east by the Cathedral. The first of these three buildings was designed by Jorge Manuel Theotocopouli, El Greco's son, at the beginning of the XVIIth century. Built in Renaissance style, it features two interesting twin towers covered with slate and crowned with spires.

The original nucleus of the Archbishop's Palace was the house of Archbishop Jiménez de Rada, built during the XIIIth century on land ceded by Alfonso VIII. It was then transformed and extended by other archbishops. The arch that joins it to the Cathedral at the height of

the Puerta de Mollete was erected by Cardinal Mendoza. It owes its present appearance to an initiative of Cardinal Lorenzana who had it demolished to give it it's present day structure. The outside façade in Neoclassic style was constructed during the XVIIIth century.

Even though the Law Court was built recently, its appearance has been adapted to successfully blend in with the square's architecture.

THE CATHEDRAL

Unlike the cathedrals in other Spanish cities such as Seville or Jaén, on which we have not only documents but also archaeological finds feeding us information as to their origins and subsequent transformations, we have no definite information on Toledo Cathedral; in

Cathedral, the Puerta del Perdón.

Cathedral, the Puerta del Reloj.

Cathedral,▶
view of the Cloister.

fact, we only have indirect references in documents dating back to that period and very slight traces of how it was possibly built in the past. We do not know which buildings existed during Roman times, even if it is assumed that they were important basilicas, temples or civic buildings near to the city's «forum». There is a lack of information on the Visigothic and Moorish settlements. Legend has it that the first temple to be built on this site was that of S. Ildefonso, patron of the city, to whom the Virgin appeared, thus rewarding him for the fervent defence of his virginity. When the city was conquered by the Arabs, the temple was converted into a mosque; in 1085 it became Christian once again thanks to Alfonso VI. It was then destroyed and in its place construction was commenced on the present

building in 1227, at the time of Ferdinand III the Saint. The new basilica is today considered one of the finest examples of XIIIth century Gothic architecture, with evident references to the French model; however the Castilian influence can be noted in that more balanced proportions replace the predominance of the vertical rhythm.

The Cathedral consists of a nave and four aisles of different widths; the nave and two central aisles are slightly narrower than the two outermost aisles. At the bottom of the temple one can admire the magnificent, grandiosely-proportioned apse which skilfully reunites different architectural themes; it is crowned by a vault featuring highly original characteristics. Around it, a series of richly decorated chapels opens up.

Cathedral, the wooden choir-stalls.

Cathedral, the eagle-shaped lectern (Vicente Salinas, 1646).

Cathedral, view of the nave. ▶

The main façade of the Cathedral, commenced in 1418, leads onto the Plaza del Ayuntamiento. It features three doors respectively known as the Tower Door or Door of Hell (to the left), Door of Pardon (in the centre), and Door of the Last Judgement or of the Scribes (to the right). The Door of Pardon was thus named on account of the custom of granting indulgences; it is only opened during the visits of Heads of State or the day in which the new Cardinal of Toledo takes possession of the cathedral. It is flanked by the apostles; the image of Christ appears in the mullioned window with two lights. The table portrays the appearance of the Virgin imposing the planet on S. Ildefonso.

Cathedral, back part of the Capilla Mayor.

Cathedral, the Gothic ▶ retablo of the high altar.

Cathedral, exterior of the Capilla Mayor and right aisle.

Cathedral, Capilla de los Reyes Nuevos: Eleanor of Aragon praying (Jorge de Contreras).

The Watch Door opens onto the Calle de la Chapine-ría or de la Feria; it dates back to the end of the XIIIth century and is the oldest of all of the doors. Various episodes of the New Testament, attributed to Juán Alemán, are depicted in its pointed arch. The watch was incorporated in the XVIth century; the present one, however, dates back to the XVIIIth century. The iconography on the organ case is by Diego Copín.

The cloister was built at the request of the Portuguese archbishop Pedro de Tenorio, the city's great patron. Work was carried out under the direction of Rodrigo Alonso in 1381. It consists of two floors built according to a perfectly square plan with five branches that coincide with those of the Cathedral's nave and aisles. The galleries are each 52 metres long. The quadripartite vaults are extremely simple and are only interrupted by the keys of the Archbishop Tenorio's coat-of arms. The ground floor houses some frescoes alluding to the saints of Toledo — Eugenio, Casilda and Eladio — attributed to Bayeu; another two frescoes representing the martyr-

Cathedral, the Mozarabic Chapel.

◄Cathedral, the «Transparent» Monument behind the Capilla Mayor.

Cathedral, Chapel of S. Ildefonso:
the tomb of the Archbishop Albornoz.

dom of S. Leocadia and S. Daciano are in turn attributed to Mariano Maella.

By standing in the nave and turning one's back on the main door, one comes face to face with the back part of the chancel, an excellent example of Gothic art. Externally this part of the chancel is flanked by three altars dedicated to S. Catalina (to the right), to the Virgin de la Estrella (in the centre) and to Christ (to the left). The internal part of the chancel is considered the most beautiful in Spain. The lower stalls, built in embossed inlay by Rodrigo Alemán during the XVth century, are decorated with scenes of the conquest of Granada by the Catholic Kings. A series of figures and animals, indicating their author's vivid imagination, are also depicted. In all there are 50 seats in walnut. The upper stalls, which are also built in walnut and are clearly in Renaissance style, total 70 seats. Alonso de Berruguete is responsible for the choirs to the right; he likewise sculpted the Transfiguration in alabaster to be found in the upper part. Those to the right were built by Felipe de Borgoña and can seat 35. Above the archbishop's

throne, one can admire an alabastre frieze once again representing the investiture of S. Ildefonso, attributed to Gregorio de Borgoña, Felipe's brother.

The chancel features some invaluable works like the marble Vergine Blanca dating back to the XIVth century. The bronze spread-eagle pulpit in the centre was done by Vicente Salinas in 1664. The two organs above the chancel tribunes are respectively called de la Epistola (in Baroque style, attributed to Germán López) and del Evangelio (in Neoclassic style).

The magnificent Capilla Mayor, containing one of the richest collections of ornaments in Spain, was transformed at the time of Cardinal Cisneros, who had the royal chapel eliminated to widen the presbytery and place inside it a larqe wooden retablo inlaid with gilded, multi-coloured ornaments. Well-known artists like Copín de Holanda, Enrique Egas, Gumiel, and others contributed to the creation of this masterpieces.

The retablo narrates scenes from the life of Jesus Christ and its central part contains an image of the Virgin Mary with Baby Jesus. To the left, one comes across

◄The Gate of the Cambrón
with Toledo's coat of arms.

Hospital de Tavera: overview.

LA PUERTA DEL CAMBRON

This Renaissance style gate was built in 1576 to replace the previous one which was built by the Visigoth king Wamba. The façade facing the city is characterized by a statue of S. Leocadia attributed to Berruguete. The other façade bears the shield with the coat-of-arms of Toledo. There are slate-roofed towers at both sides and fragments of Roman and Arab buildings are incorporated in the tower itself.

TAVERA HOSPITAL

This hospital was founded in 1541 by Juan Pardo de Tavera, Archbishop of Toledo and General Inquisitor. It is situated in front of the Gate of Bisagra, which is why it is also known as the «Hospital de Afuera». The works ended in 1603 and famous architects contributed to its construction, from Bustamante to Covarrubias and from González de Lara to Vergara. The outside walls were completed during the XVIIIth century. The style is Renaissance with echoes of Florentine palaces. The three-storey façade is built of granite.

The courtyard is divided by a corridor which crosses it from the entrance to the church dedicated to St. John the Baptist, whose door in Carrara marble is attributed to Berruguete. It consists of only a nave; the plan is a Roman cross, in the centre of which is the tomb of the cardinal who founded the building, also attributed to Berruguete. In the underground crypts, members of the families of the Dukes of Lerma and Medinaceli are buried.

The west wing of the hospital was transformed into a palace by the Duke of Lerma during the XVIIth century and into a museum in 1940 by the homonymous foundation. This palace is the emblem of all the splendour of the high society of that era and contains valuable works pertaining to its museological collection and which are distributed among its various rooms. In the dining-hall, one can admire an equestrian portrait of the Emperor Charles V, painted by Sánchez Coello, as well as other paintings of nobles of that period. The Archives not only house all the documents relating to the building of the hospital but also exhibit «The Holy Family» by El Greco, not to mention «The Philosopher» and the discussed «La Mujer Barbuda» or «Bearded Woman», both by Ribera. In the room called Greco one can admire the portrait of Cardinal Tavera, built according to the model of the prelate's death-mask, «St. Peter's Tears» and «St. Francis»; it is most definitely worth tak-

Hospital de Tavera: the patio.

Hospital de Tavera: Museum of the Duchess of
Lerma: the Holy Family by El Greco.

Hospital de Tavera, Museum of the Duchess of Lerma: ▶
the Archives and the Duchess's bedroom.

ing a look at «Christ's Baptism» on account of the
magnificence of the unusual colours and dimensions. El
Greco's works are displayed alongside portraits of aris-
tocrats of that period painted by Zurbarán and
Bartolomé González and two tapestries of the XVIth
and XVIIth centuries. The duchess's bedrooms houses
various paintings: Tintoretto's «Holy Family», two
works by Luca Giordano — «St. Gregory's Mass» and
«The Prayer in the Vegetable Garden» — and another
painting from the Italian school, «Jesus, Martha and
Mary», together with a Gothic crucifix above the
bedhead. The duke's room contains a portrait of the last
descendant of the Lermas, painted by Sotomayor, and
another portrait of the mother, the Duchess of
Medinaceli, achieved by Edouard Dubufé in 1861. A
point of interest in this room is created by the small
painting of the Flemish school depicting a shipwreck
caused by demons. Of the furniture, it is worth noting
the ebony and ivory cabinet portraying various scenes
from the bible. Lastly, in the chapel's vestibule, one can
admire a painting by Snyders with hunting scenes. It is
also interesting to visit the pharmacy dating back to the
XVIIth century where period instruments are kept.

THE NEW GATE OF BISAGRA

This is the city's most famous gate and the one encountered when coming from Madrid; it dates back to 1550. To the sides of the tower itself and on the outside are two imposing towers equipped with loopholes for defence purposes that almost reach ground level. On the gate one can admire an enormous frieze in granite portraying a two-headed eagle. Above they built a pediment crowned by an angel who keeps guard over the city, brandishing a sword. The façade facing the city one again bears the coat-of-arms of Toledo and to the sides it features two square towers crowned with two pyramidal domes covered with green and white tiles. It is the work of the maestro Covarrubias. According to some authors the name of this gate

The Cristo de la Vega kept in the Church of S. Leocadia, built on the site of a Visigoth basilica.

The strong Puerta Nueva de Bisagra.

Two pictures of the Puerta Vieja de Bisagra, also known as the Gate of Alfonso VI.

could come from *via sacra*, with the inhabitants of Toledo emulating the homonymous street in Rome. Another theory maintains that the name is originally Arab: «bab» meaning gate and «shara» meaning red; what gave rise to this theory is the presence of red clays towards the north of the city.

THE OLD GATE OF BISAGRA OR OF ALFONSO VI

It is generally believed that this gate was built at the beginning of the IXth century. Arab art is present in the lower part and Moorish architecture in the upper part. Tradition has it that that Alfonso VI entered through this gate after his troops had reconquered the city on the 25th May 1085.

Church of Santiago de Arrabal: the exterior.

Church of Santiago de Arrabal: ▶ the interior.

THE CHURCH OF SANTIAGO DE ARRABAL

It would appear that this temple was built on the site where a mosque originally stood. As in the case of many other churches in Toledo, this church was commissioned by Alfonso VI. A peculiarity of this church is its bell-tower completely detached from the rest of the building, which is an uncommon sight in Spain. It consists of a nave and two aisles where stone and decorative brick alternate, creating an appearance of placid sobriety. It is worth noting the XIVth century pulpit in the left aisle, which is famous because it was where S. Vicente Ferrer delivered his fervent sermons thanks to which he managed to convert numerous Jews to the Roman faith. The restored work of the high altar portrays the apostle Santiago in the centre.

◄The Puerta del Sol.

The Church of Cristo de la Luz,
already a mosque.

LA PUERTA DEL SOL

This Moorish gate is to be found near the Gate of Bisagra at the end of the Calle Real del Arrabal and in the direction of Zocodover Square. Like many other typical buildings in Toledo, it is built in stone and brick. It was constructed at the time of Archbishop Tenorio and it is presumed that it was used as the main entrance to the city. It consists of two fortified towers which differ one from the other as the left one is round while the right one is square. The central body is in stone, whereas the ornamental battlements are in brick. Two stone columns support the main pointed arch.

The marble shield above the access arch one again represents the Virgin Mary imposing the planet on S. Ildefonso. In the upper part of the shield the sun and moon are portrayed, indicating the city's interest in astronomy and science, possibly giving rise to the name of the gate itself. An unusual iconograph is to be found in the centre: two women holding a tray on which a man's head rests. It is generally believed that the head belonged to a certain Fernando González, a town officer, who used violence against two young women; Ferdinand III the Saint therefore obtained his beheadal and insisted that the scene be immortalized in stone to act as a public warning.

THE MOSQUE OF CRISTO DE LA LUZ

Originally this temple was probably a place of prayer and worship for the Visigoths; it is thought to have been founded by Atanagildo. It was transformed and converted into a mosque by the invading Moors and then trans-

121

◄ *The Church of Cristo de la Luz: the typical horse-shoe shaped arches of the interior.*

The dome with Spanish-Moorish decorations dating back to the XVth century of the church of the Convento de la Concepcíon.

formed into a Christian church once again after the reconquest of Toledo by Alfonso VI, who had a mass officiated here as thanksgiving for his victory over the pagans.

The three arches of the doors of the internal façade are all different and are accompanied by a series of intertwined arches. An Arab engraving reads: ONLY ALLAH IS GREAT. Indoors two areas can be distinguished. The first, at the entrance, is a square with a series of columns crowned by domes, which are all different and which rest on walls and pillars, four of which have Visigoth capitals. The second part is in Moorish style and contains frescoes of the XIIIth century in a precarious state of repair.

*A picture of the Castle of San Servando,
at the foot of which stands
the Alcántara bridge.*

THE CASTLE OF S. SERVANDO

This castle stands on a hill in front of the Alcántara bridge. On this site stood a fortification built in Roman times; the oldest parts of the existing building were, however, erected by the Moors. It was completely restored by Alfonso VI after the reconquest of the city and was always used as a bulwark for the defence of the left side of the river. Some sources maintain that El Cid Campeador was appointed governor of the castle; it was then handed over to the Knight Templars. Other sources support the theory that Alfonso VI built it and gave it to the Cluny monks whose convent was in the vicinity of the castle. It was abandoned during the XIIth century as a result of repeated attacks by the Moors. It was seriously damaged during the war between Pedro the Cruel and his brother Enrique de Trastámara. In 1945 the castle was handed over to the «Delegación de Juventudes», who restored it and converted it into a school.

San Juan de Dios, a typical alley in Toledo.

THE STREETS OF TOLEDO

Walking along the streets of Toledo means walking through Visigoth, Mohammedan and Jewish Spain. The vast majority of these streets stand out on account of their curves, narrowness and abundance of monuments. Toledo has changed very little over the past four centuries managing to preserve its churches, houses, walls and buildings. Some streets narrow all of a sudden and sometimes are linked to others through flights of steps; this blocks traffic but facilitates tourists sparing them long walks in search of places of historic and artistic interest. Often the names of the streets bear witness to past traditions and legends, activities and customs.

The name of the Calle de los Alfileritos, for example, comes from an old custom. At number 24 one can observe an alcove with a statue of the Virgin Mary in front of which the young maidens to be married used to press their large, coloured hairpins into their hair having pricked themselves slightly in the hopes of obtaining the Virgin Mary's protection in their search for the husband of their dreams. Legend has it that this custom dates back to the XVIth century, when a noble lady, separated from her loved one as he had gone to war with Charles V, prayed to the Virgin Mary day and night for the return of her knight. When she could no longer keep awake, her lady-in-waiting, had orders to prick her with one of her pins which at daybreak was offered to the Virgin Mary as a sign of the sacrifice of numerous nightwatches. After many years of hopeful waiting, the knight returned safe and sound, giving credit to the belief that this Virgin Mary listened to the prayers of the young sweethearts.

The Calle del Hombre del Palo or «street of the man with the wooden stick» is thus named because one day an engineer, none other than Charles V's watchmaker — Juanelo Turriano — presented in public a wooden machine with human features and made it walk along this very road.

Some of the best local handicrafts shops line Calle de San Juan de Dios. These shops usually exhibit their merchandise on the outside walls of their houses.

*Some significant examples of local
handicraft production: pottery and swords.*

HANDICRAFTS IN TOLEDO

Local handicrafts can be roughly divided into four main activities that occupy the vast majority of the local population: ceramics, sword manufacture, damascening and the production of Toledo's most typical sweet: marzipan. Toledo's swords and daggers are world famous. For example, every year at the Academia General Militar del Cile the best cadet officer is ceremoniously awarded a sabre manufactured here by the Head of State. Having visited the city and appreciated the elegance and skill with which these swords are manufactured, tourists often yield to temptation and buy one as a souvenir of their stay in Toledo.

These swords are handmade according to procedures and techniques that have been handed down from father to son for countless generations. They start off as nothing more than a piece of steel, which is then forged, hardened, hammered and flattened until the required thickness is obtained. They are then cooled in

large water containers before being smoked for a matter of minutes to obtain that typical blue-grey colour; in this way one obtains the blade to which the hilt is then welded. At this stage, all that remains to be done is to is impress the colours with special paints, a task that requires extreme dexterity because of the attention required in impressing even the most minute details.

From some points of view, damascening is very similar to sword manufacture: a steel blade is encrusted with gold filigree and then treated with special enamels to obtain diversified, elegant patterns on a wide range of objects.

Today's ceramic industry owes its abundance of themes and technical skill to the fusion of elements of the three cultures that meet here. The result of this artistic integration is what is currently known as Moorish style which, combining precision and dexterity in the use of colour, gives rise to highly decorative architectural elements and ornamental household goods.

The marzipan is prepared with almonds and sugar. Toledo's industries stand out because of their refined, elegant wrappings. The word «mazapán» probably comes from the Arab custom to preserve sweets and spices in special boxes called *mahasaban* in Arabic.

CONTENTS